WARRIOR SOCIETIES
A Manifesto

WARRIOR SOCIETIES

A Manifesto

ROBERTA CAROL HARVEY
A Citizen of the Navajo Nation

SUNSTONE
PRESS

SANTA FE

Sunstone books may be purchased for educational, business, or sales promotional use.
For information please write: Special Markets Department, Sunstone Press,
P.O. Box 2321, Santa Fe, New Mexico 87504-2321.
Printed on acid-free paper
∞

Library of Congress Cataloging-in-Publication Data

Names: Harvey, Roberta Carol, 1950- author.
Title: Warrior societies : a manifesto / Roberta Carol Harvey, Dine
   (Navajo Nation) citizen.
Description: Santa Fe : Sunstone Press, [2023] | Summary: "In the past,
   American Indian War Societies possessed the highest moral obligation and
   duty for the continued survival of Indian peoples and their strong and
   vibrant future; given our current state of war, they need to be
   revived"-- Provided by publisher.
Identifiers: LCCN 2023054286 | ISBN 9781632936523 (paperback) | ISBN
   9781632936516 (hardback) | ISBN 9781611397338 (epub)
Subjects: LCSH: Indigenous peoples--Cultural assimilation--United States. |
   Cultural property--Destruction and pillage--United States. | Cultural
   property--Repatriation--United States.
Classification: LCC E98.C89 H37 2023 | DDC 323.1197--dc23/eng/20231222
LC record available at https://lccn.loc.gov/2023054286

WWW.SUNSTONEPRESS.COM
SUNSTONE PRESS / POST OFFICE BOX 2321 / SANTA FE, NM 87504-2321 /USA
(505) 988-4418

To My Sons, D.J. and Aaron
For Their Pride, Discipline, Guardianship and Commitment to
Their Families, Native Identity and Communities

Acknowledgments

My Family

Nobody is more helpful to me than the members of my family. They continue to encourage me and ensure that whatever resources I need for my research and writing are available. Thank you to my most beloved husband for his active support of my advocacy for indigenous peoples.

CONTENTS

Preface // 9

Warrior Societies Manifesto // 11

Case Study No. 1: Doctrine of Discovery // 13

Case Study No. 2: The Starving Rabbit // 17

Case Study No. 3: "Whiskey Is for Drinking, Water Is for Fighting" // 19

Case Study No. 4: The White Shoe Law Firm // 21

Case Study No. 5: "This Isn't the 15th Century" // 23

Case Study No. 6: The 'Lost' Shoreline // 25

Case Study No. 7: Last Arrow // 27

Case Study No. 8: Skull Studies // 29

Case Study No. 9: Get Money Up Front // 33

Case Study No. 10: Condemned Bacon // 35

Case Study No. 11: Utes Thrown Out of Colorado due to Meeker and Major Thornburgh // 37

Case Study No. 12: "If You're Not at the Table, You're on the Menu" // 39

Case Study No. 13: Low Ball // 41

Case Study No. 14: Polishing a Diamond // 43

Case Study No. 15: Throwaway Treaty // 45

Case Study No. 16: Land Sharks // 47

Case Study No. 17: Mayhem // 49

Case Study No. 18: Beware the Commissioner: Cheyenne and Arapaho Thrown Out of Colorado // 51

Case Study No. 19: "The Lobo" // 53

Case Study No. 20: Fake Friends // 55

Case Study No. 21: Knights of the Forest // 57

Case Study No. 22: One Treaty Provision Permitted Transcontinental Railroad // 59

Case Study No. 23: Up Against the Wall // 63

Case Study No. 24: Indoctrination // 67

Case Study No. 25: The Iron Triangle // 69

Conclusion // 75

Notes: Warrior Societies' Manifesto // 77

Preface

After researching Indian history, the patterns of destructive governmental practices endured by Indian Nations are obvious. Many others have written and spoken about this. Kevin Gover, Assistant Secretary-Indian Affairs, Department of the Interior, at the Ceremony Acknowledging the 175th Anniversary of the Establishment of the Bureau of Indian Affairs, September 8, 2000, specifically addressed these patterns: "the deliberate spread of disease, the decimation of the mighty bison herds, the use of the poison alcohol to destroy mind and body, and the cowardly killing of women and children..."

The Final Report of a First Nation Research Project on Healing in Canadian Aboriginal Communities, APC 21 CA in 2002, by the Solicitor General, MAPPING THE HEALING JOURNEY, addressed the same horror of abuses resulting from colonization, including:
The destruction of traditional economies through the expropriation of traditional lands and resources; The undermining of traditional identity, spirituality, language and culture through missionization, residential schools and government day schools; and The destruction of indigenous forms of governance, community organization and community cohesion.

Maria Yellow Horse Brave Heart, PhD, and Lemyra M. DeBruyn, PhD, in their studies of The American Indian Holocaust: Healing Historical Unresolved Grief, concluded similarly the historical unresolved grief of Indian peoples originates "from the loss of lives, land, and vital aspects of Native culture promulgated by the European conquest of the Americas."

I know that we are smart, brave, strong and resilient. Our purpose now is to ensure the vitality of Indian Nations. I honor those on the forefront protecting our lives, land and rights. In the past, our War Societies were tasked with ensuring their people's survival during times of war. It is time to admit that we are at war and that these disciplined, sober Societies must be revived. We need the physical and mental strength, the confident and resolute conviction, the education and connection to our Indian identities, the leadership and protection of our Nations by our Warrior Class. I am proud to be Diné and I know I am not alone.

WARRIOR SOCIETIES MANIFESTO

The primary function of the United States is to protect its territorial integrity and sovereignty over its claimed lands, resources, and population, which includes Indian lands which they hold in trust, with authority over Indians as citizens. As stated by United States General John Pope in 1878: "It is absolutely imperative that Indian Nations realize the United States' premeditated and calculated determination of "*the dispossession of the savage and the occupation of the lands by civilized man*" and that "*it is certain that the larger part of the country claimed by him will, in some manner, pass into the possession of the white race.*"[1]

Warrior Societies

Warrior societies should be activated to protect Indian sovereignty, with the organization, leadership, training and discipline to embody the patience, persistence and ruthlessness needed to protect Indian land and resources.

Case Studies for Tribal Leaders

As a tribal leader, the following historical examples are provided for your consideration. The Notes section has history related to each Case Study.

Dispossessing Indians of Land and Resources

Dispossessing Indians of their land and resources followed a common trajectory. It started with the legal fiction that Indians didn't own their land, but were mere tenants at sufferance, permitting their ouster from their land. If they were tenants, they didn't own the natural resources on their lands.

The tactics to accomplish this dispossession included intimidation, lying, stealing, cheating, harassing, trespassing, fraud, mispresenting the value of Indian land and resources, removal, extermination, massacres, private wars funded by the federal government, war crimes, massive cession of lands, concentration and consolidation of Indians on reservations, allotment of tribal land to individuals to break up the tribal mass, alienability of allotments and termination. Repudiating the sovereignty of Indian Nations and assimilating Indians into the body politic wasn't questioned. These practices were endorsed by the President, the executive branch, the military, Congress and the judiciary. With this impetus, states selected their own method for securing for their citizens the inexhaustible mineral, agricultural, water and natural resources within their dominion. Big business used its political and economic clout to assure its imperial control of the country's natural wealth. Settlers were the boots-on-the-ground.

The true purpose of removal wasn't humanitarian; it was about moving a perceived obstacle out of the way of the westward expansion of settlers. It was about control of the west's immense and valuable natural resources, which would benefit the (1) U.S. Treasury; (2) economy; (3) industrial tycoons; (4) timber barons; (5) mineral magnates; and (6) capital investors. They were aware of the value of the land on which the diminishing timber, gold, fertile soil, water and oil abounded. The outright, blatant theft of resources would be facilitated by the government exercising militant control of the Indians. If they were in a limited, prescribed area that control would be easier. Whenever an Indian Nation offered any resistance, the Interior Department transferred its authority over that Nation to the War Department.

Given any major economic upheaval, the Iron Triangle of the government, big business and the colonial white settlers will conjure up a justification once more and turn for its rescue to Indian land and resources. Be aware of the instant water shortage and the lack of federal funding for the infrastructure necessary to deliver water to Indian communities. Also, the continuing tension between Indian Nations and states is but the continuing issue of an 'imperium in imperio.' No state wants another state within its boundaries.

CASE STUDY NO. 1: DOCTRINE OF DISCOVERY

In 1991, University of Oklahoma Law Professor Lindsay G. Robertson found *fifty years* of corporate records of the United Land Company documenting the collusive effort to confirm title to the Indian lands it purchased from tribes. The United Land Company planned and funded the *Johnson v. M'Intosh* litigation for the prosecution and the defense.[2] Three Presidential Cabinet members knew the case was fraudulent and did nothing.

The Chief Justice, John Marshall, had 240 square miles of family-owned land purchased under state law at stake. Even though he had an undeniable conflict of interest in the outcome of the case, he failed to recuse himself from hearing the case. Justice James Wilson also had a vested interest in the case and similarly failed to recuse himself. As President of the United Land Company in 1780, he was the largest single investor with an interest totaling over 1,000,000 acres.

Without citing any legal authority for his decision, Chief Justice Marshall held that, under the European 'doctrine of discovery,' the land discovered in the 'New World' belonged to the 'discovering' sovereign, so long as there was no Christian sovereign or populace. The thirteen states, having defeated Great Britain in the American Revolution, alleged they succeeded to its title which was based on the 'doctrine of discovery.'

The U.S. claimed France's 'doctrine of discovery' title in the Louisiana Purchase. It alleged it succeeded to Spain/Mexico's 'discovery' claim of the Southwest by conquest. It made its own discovery claim of the Pacific Northwest based on military expeditions and Treaties with Russia and Spain to acquire their 'discovery' claims.

The 'doctrine of discovery' promulgated for the United States by Chief Justice Marshall was as follows:

> They (Indians) were admitted to be the rightful occupants of the soil, with a legal as well as just claim to retain possession of it, and to use it according to their own discretion; but their rights to complete sovereignty as independent nations were necessarily diminished, and their power to dispose of the soil at their own will to whomsoever they pleased was denied by the original fundamental principle that *discovery gave exclusive title to those who made it*. (Emphasis added).[3]

Censoring Chief Justice Marshall

Chief Justice Marshall went far beyond the facts when the case should have been decided by simply determining the title between the plaintiff and defendant. Three months after the *Johnson* decision, Thomas Jefferson complained to Justice William Johnson: "This practice of Judge Marshall, of travelling out of his case to prescribe what the law would be in a moot case not before the court, is very irregular and very censurable."[4]

Vatican Repudiates 'Doctrine of Discovery;' It Must Annul All Underlying Bulls

The Vatican issued the following statement on March 30, 2023, *repudiating* the 'doctrine of discovery':

> The legal concept of "discovery" was debated by colonial powers from the sixteenth century onward and found particular expression in the nineteenth century jurisprudence of courts in several countries, according to which the discovery of lands by settlers granted an exclusive right to extinguish, either by purchase or conquest, the title to or possession of those lands by indigenous peoples. Certain scholars have argued that the basis of the aforementioned "doctrine" is to be found in several

papal documents, such as the Bulls *Dum Diversas* (1452), *Romanus Pontifex* (1455) and *Inter Caetera* (1493). ... The Catholic Church therefore **repudiates** those concepts that fail to recognize the inherent human rights of indigenous peoples, including what has become known as the legal and political "doctrine of discovery." (Emphasis added).[5]

Annul All Underlying Bulls

It is not enough for the Vatican to repudiate the 'concept' of the Doctrine of Discovery; it must **annul** all of the underlying Bulls - Dum Diversas, Romanus Pontifex and Inter Caetera and all other related Bulls. In the past the Church used the words *"null, and void of all validity for ever"*, to reverse a position, not repudiate. The word "repudiates" is ambiguous and does not have a set meaning.

Book I of the Catholic Church's Code of Canon Law contains general norms that govern the nature and application of ecclesiastical laws and processes. Canons 7-34, in particular, provide insight into the nature and interpretation of laws. ... An illustration of the importance of these "laws governing laws" is exemplified in Canon 10: *"Only those laws must be considered invalidating or disqualifying which expressly establish that an act is null or that a person is unqualified."* (Emphasis added). Canon 10 states that an invalidating law renders the act performed null and void; the action performed does not exist in the eyes of the church.[6]

Catholic Church Must Accept Full Accountability for Abuses

The Catholic Church must accept full accountability for the abuses by competing colonial powers acting under its AUTHORITY. The Church may not distance itself from acknowledging its actual culpability in the abuses that occurred, which it is still doing. We can't be fooled by smoke and mirrors.

Catholic Church's Infallibility

The Catholic Church's infallibility was proclaimed in 1090 by Pope Gregory VII in Dictatus Papae, The Dictates of the Pope: "*That the Roman church has never erred; nor will it err to all eternity, the Scripture bearing witness.*" This is why the language of the Vatican itself when it wishes to repudiate prior doctrine requires it to declare a Bull null and void through the issuance of a Papal Bull, not a mere repudiation.

> When Pope Alexander VI in the Bull *Inter Caetera* invoked "*the fullness of our apostolic power, by the authority of Almighty God conferred upon us in blessed Peter and of the vicarship of Jesus Christ, which we hold on earth*," he spoke *ex cathedra* as spiritual head of the Church universal and in this capacity the bull is vested with the authority of the infallibility of the pope on questions so designated. His stated intent is to bind the church universal under pain of incurring *naufragium fideli*, or spiritual shipwreck ... (Emphasis added).[7]

The Bull contained the following admonishment for violating *Inter Caetera* - the wrath of Almighty God:

> "Let no one, therefore, infringe, or with rash boldness contravene, this our recommendation, exhortation, requisition, gift, grant, assignment, constitution, deputation, decree, mandate, prohibition, and will. Should anyone presume to attempt this, be it known to him that he will incur the wrath of Almighty God and of the blessed apostles Peter and Paul."[8]

CASE STUDY NO. 2: THE STARVING RABBIT

On January 2, 2023, Montana Republican State Senator Keith Regier proposed a draft resolution to Congress arguing that the "Indian reservation system is a policy based solely on race, which is diametrically opposed to both the United States Constitution and the Constitution of the state of Montana." Further, he stated the continuation of the reservation system is not in the best interests of the state or the Indians.[9]

State Senator Regier's present day proposal is not that much different from Arizona's in 1885. The Territorial Legislature petitioned Congress for all Apache lands, asserting, that they were occupying the richest mineral, agricultural and timber lands of the Territory, had made no use of said lands, but were simply withholding them from public use and occupation, and were a perpetual menace to the peaceful settler, retarding progress, paralyzing prosperity ...[10]

Truth about Quality of Indian Lands

In 1916, Com'r Cato Sell's revealed the truth about Indian allotments consigned to Indian families:

> *I know of many allotments depending entirely upon which an Indian family would starve to death* ... There are thousands of acres of land on Indian reservations where 100 hundred acres would not feed a rabbit. ... (Emphasis added).[11]

Comment: It is imperative that Indian Nations prepare for these types of threats to their sovereignty. With drawn out inflation and water scarcity, more of these challenges may arise.

Case Study No. 3: "Whiskey Is for Drinking, Water Is for Fighting"

The real battle in mining was over the water, scarce in the desert and made even more valuable by the high stakes of gold mining. When water was scarce, mercury had to be used to separate the gold, but this method was considerably more expensive. It cost more than most miners could afford, thus, placing a premium on water. As *in western agriculture and ranching, whoever controlled the water supply controlled production, in this case, of gold*. Mark Twain's adage, "Whiskey's for drinking, water's for fighting," would be played out in the arid west.

In 1876, the DOI reported on the lack of water for farming for Indians in eastern Nevada: *the water used for irrigating purposes has been taken from them, and their crops have dried up and become worthless.* (Emphasis added).[12] This story was repeated over and over across Indian country.

Comment: Current Water Scarcity - Indian Nations – Be Vigilant

From past experience any of the following may be tried: an angle, bait and switch, con, conspiracy, deception, device, distortion, fraud, gimmick, maneuver, plot, ploy, ruse, artifice, chicanery, double-dealing, duplicity, machination, pretense, snare, subterfuge, treachery, etc.

CASE STUDY NO. 4: THE WHITE SHOE LAW FIRM

On June 29, 2022, the U.S. Supreme Court decision in *Oklahoma v. Castro-Huerta*, 142 S. Ct. 2486 (2022), held that "the Federal Government and the State have concurrent jurisdiction to prosecute crimes committed by non-Indians against Indians in Indian country." The Court, in a 5-4 decision, overturned the long-held understanding that states do not have this authority.

Zachary C. Schauf, arguing his first case before the U.S. Supreme Court, alluded to two key litigation problems facing Indian Nations:

> 1. In many cases, Indian Nations are *unable to retain lawyers with the necessary caliber of experience*. As stated by Schauf, the State of Oklahoma retained "*a white shoe NY law firm*" to represent it. A "white shoe firm" is a term for the most prestigious, well-established businesses and companies. Kannon Shanmugam, counsel for the State of Oklahoma, had argued *35 cases before the Supreme Court*, including 15 cases in the last five years. His going rate was *$1,824/hour, which he cut in half for the State.*

> 2. In many cases, Indian Nations lack the ability to compensate lawyers at the rates charged by white shoe law firms. Oklahoma paid *$1.4 million to its law firm which agreed to bill the state at 50% of its normal rate.*[13]

In most cases, companies, with the same issues at stake, will form a litigation committee, *pool their financial resources* and legal expertise and retain a "*a white shoe law firm*" to represent them. They understand the importance of retaining quality legal counsel. By pooling their financial resources, they lessen the cost for each company participating. By pooling the legal expertise of the litigation committee, they bring to bear a group of lawyers well-versed in their area of the law. They are patient and persistent. For example, Oklahoma will not give up its efforts to set aside *McGirt v. Oklahoma*. It will bide its time and wait for the right facts to present themselves. Remember that the plaintiffs in *Johnson v. M'Intosh* waited 50 years and had no qualms in repeatedly seeking Congressional assistance to support its position.

Indian Nations Must Build Litigation War Chests and Pool Their Financial and Legal Resources to Obtain "White Shoe Firm" Representation

Indian Nations must pool their resources to obtain the same legal advantages of their opponents. ***Regardless of the Castro-Huerta decision,*** Indian Nations ***must continue to build the capacity of their tribal justice systems which are the guardians of tribal sovereignty. The Navajo Nation is considering establishing a law school to train lawyers who will be knowledgeable with its codes and traditional practices. This should be given the highest priority for the Nation.***

CASE STUDY NO. 5: "THIS ISN'T THE 15TH CENTURY"

The Northwest Passage Sea Route, which links northern Europe to northeast Asia, is just one of three passages that Arctic countries and a host of non-polar nations are hoping to exploit. Scientists predict the Northwest Passage will be largely ice free by 2050 if current levels of warming continue.[14] "China knows that the potential for shipping is profound. A vessel heading for Europe from Shanghai could cut several thousand kilometres off the southern route by using the Arctic waterway instead, which would represent a huge cost-saving." Ahead of meetings by the Arctic Council, a group of nations that border the area raised suspicions about China's ambitions for the region and slammed Russia's "pattern of aggressive behaviour" there—and took a swing at Canada.[15] Aqqaluq Lynge, speaking for the Arctic Indigenous Peoples' Caucus before the United Nations reminded them: *"The world needs to know that the Arctic is already inhabited; it is not a scientific laboratory; it is not a museum. It is our home."* (Emphasis added).[16]

Russia is purportedly preparing a "doctrine of discovery" claim to the estimated ten billion tons of oil and gas underlying the Arctic Ocean by having planted its titanium flag on the floor of the Ocean in 2007. This flag planting ploy, an element of the European 'doctrine of discovery,' concerned Canada's Foreign Minister, Peter MacKay, who stated: *"This isn't the 15th century. You can't go around the world and just plant flags and say: 'We're claiming this territory.'"* (Emphasis added).[17] As climate change impacts land bases, the world's imperial countries plan to use the Doctrine of Discovery to claim new land areas uncovered by receding waters, even if claimed by indigenous peoples.

Comment: Don't allow any flag planting or accept any Loyalty Certificates.

Case Study No. 6: The 'Lost' Shoreline

In 1947, the U.S. Army Corps of Engineers ("Army Corps") flooded a large portion of the Fort Berthold Reservation in North Dakota. In tears, Council Chairman George Gillette "consented" to the coercive legislation authorizing the construction. "The truth is, as everyone knows," he said, "our Treaty of Fort Laramie...and our constitution are being torn to shreds by this contract."

At the time the Garrison Dam and Reservoir Project eliminated the Three Affiliated Tribes ("TAT") use of the shoreland, *WHAT WAS BEING FORFEITED WAS NOT EXPLAINED TO OR UNDERSTOOD BY TAT*. In 1947, TAT had no idea of the value of the shoreland for future economic development – for resorts, casinos, etc. Yet, *the DOI and the Army Corps knew of this value.* The Army Corps was charging fees for grazing, recreational and business uses of the Dam Project area.

1962 - TAT Petitions for Grazing on Garrison Dam Shoreline – Legislation Required

When TAT petitioned, in *1962,* for the *restoration of mere grazing rights* on the shoreland, legislation was required. The **FINAL LEGISLATION authorized (1)** *the right of the U.S. to control the lands* acquired within the Fort Berthold Reservation for the Garrison Dam; (2) gave the TAT a permit, which is revocable, not a right, to graze stock without charge; and (3) the right of the *Secretary of the Army to determine* what land could be used.[18]

TAT Seeking Profit Sharing from Growing Tourist Industry and Tribal Control Over Shoreline

TAT must now seek additional federal legislation to broaden its control over the shoreline. As Tribal Chairman Lone Fight has remarked: When the Garrison Dam was built the Corps' concerns were flood control and hydroelectric-power ... [but] ***Corps [officials] are just land brokers...high geared real estate brokers***. (Emphasis added).[19]

Importance of Legal Counsel

The wording used in any document whatsoever must be reviewed to determine the ***motivation*** for the ***present and future***. The government has repeatedly isolated Indian leaders to get agreements it wanted. Indian leaders must avoid this ruse by including legal counsel at all meetings, dinners, golf outings, trips to Las Vegas or other cities, etc.

CASE STUDY NO. 7: LAST ARROW

In 1890, the DOI said it was the settled policy of the Government to break up reservations, destroy tribal relations, settle Indians upon their own homesteads, incorporate them into the national life, and deal with them not as nations or tribes or bands, but as individual citizens. The proposed Indian Citizenship Act used the term "full" citizen but the Senate deleted the word "full." The draft bill permitted the Secretary of Interior to grant citizenship to those Indians who *applied*, but this was removed by the Senate. So, without consultation with Indians, the U.S. simply imposed citizenship on them. Under the **BIA Citizenship Ceremony, Indians were stripped of their Indian identity. See the Text in the Notes.**[20]

Chief Old Dog 1851–1928

When citizenship was offered Hidatsa Chief Old Dog, he declined. "I do not want the white man's offer of citizenship. I have lived a long life, and I have seen many of the Great White Fathers' promises vanish on the winds. I do not need the white man's government to tell me that I am free."[21]

Indian Citizenship Act - Plenary Act of Congress

The Indian Citizenship Act was upheld when an Onondaga Indian challenged it in 1941. The Court of Appeals for the Second Circuit said the Act was binding, even if a treaty provided otherwise.[22]

Comment: My son asked me, "If we aren't "full" citizens, what are we?"

CASE STUDY NO. 8: SKULL STUDIES

In 1905, the White Earth Reservation, comprising 750,000 acres in northwestern Minnesota, belonged to the Ojibwe Indians residing there, either as individual allottees or as property held in trust for them by the federal government.

How to Steal Indian Lands

The influence of the DOI and big business resulted in incremental Congressional legislation over five years, from 1902-1907, dismantling the Reservation. The combination of logging companies, bankers, mortgage companies, wealthy investors and attorneys stood to make a bundle of cash from the timber.

Stage Was Set to 'Get Rich Quick' Off of Indian Land

Anthropologist Warren Moorehead's first-person account discloses the confederation behind the scenes to 'get rich quick' off of Indian timber and arable land:

> The effect of the allotment on the Whites near White
> Earth was immediate. Mushroom banks sprang up in the
> surrounding small towns. The Indians in their affidavits (of
> which Linnen and myself took 505) testified that lawyers,
> banks, county officials, and business men of prominence in
> Detroit, Ogema, Mahnomen, and other towns, joined in
> the scramble to secure their pine lands and farm tracts...
> in the majority of cases, as the Indian could neither write

nor read, he did not know whether he was signing receipts, mortgages, deeds or releases.[23]

In tandem with Moorehead, contemporary historian William Folwell reported:

> Purchases from adult mixed-bloods might be strictly legal, even though they were not equitable; but fullbloods and minors were not legally competent to sell. In utter violation of law, land sharks from near and far bought allotments of full-bloods and took their deeds and had them recorded. ... Some operators did not scruple to obtain conveyances from minors ... Ignorant Indians were fleeced.[24]

Cat's Out of the Bag

On July 18, 1906, a Minneapolis newspaper reported that land speculators were plying the Indians with liquor in order to secure deeds or mortgages to their lands for small amounts; that the town had been filled with drunken Indians; and that 250 allotment mortgages had been filed at Detroit and many more in Norman County.

> Indian Commissioner R. G. Valentine ordered an investigation. Fully ninety per cent of the allotments to full-bloods had been sold or mortgaged and **eighty per cent of the whole acreage of the reservation had passed into private hands**. Full-bloods had received not more than ten per cent of the value of their land and timber. (Emphasis added).[25]

In 1911, the Commissioner of Indian Affairs reported that:

> Complete success means the recovery of 142,000 acres, valued at over $2,000,000, and for timber valued at $1,755,000, on behalf of more than 1,700 Indians, forming almost 34 per cent of the White Earth allottees.[26]

The timber industry retained attorney Ransom Powell. *First*, he used the easiest and strongest defense of all: delay. Documents get lost; memories fade; witnesses can't be located; government attorneys turn over frequently versus having an attorney handling one issue for the long run; and parties give up. *Second*, he needed to establish mixed blood status since (a) they had the right to sell their allotments; and (b) they presented the majority of the cases. *Third*, knowing that most Indians didn't have the money to bring a case, he pursued a novel theory: the federal government didn't have the right to represent individual Indian defendants since they had a state court forum for their fraud cases and he won the case he filed.

Skull Studies

In 1914 with timber-company funds, Powell hired two anthropologists for the identification of Ojibwe full-bloods and mixed-bloods. Dr. Albert E. Jenks, a professor at the University of Minnesota, and Dr. Ales Hrdlicka examined 696 Ojibwe who claimed to be full bloods, comparing their physical attributes to the Pima Indians of the southwestern United States, whom the anthropologists considered the most racially "pure" American Indians. They carefully measured and calibrated hair, eyes, nails, gums, head shapes, and teeth of White Earth Ojibwe and compared this data to measurements of the Pima.[27] Their studies narrowed the pool of full-bloods. *Of the 5,173 White Earth allottees, only 408 were considered to be full bloods - and 306 of them died before the roll was finalized in 1920*. Based on the government studies, in 1920, there were only *102 full-blood White Earth Ojibwes*. The results of this study still stand today given Judge Page Morris, Senior Judge of the United States District Court for the District of Minnesota, approving the roll and placing it on file with the Clerk of Court in Fergus Falls, Minnesota. In *Bisek v. Bellanger*, 5 F.2d 994, 995 (D. Minn. 1925), the "Blood Roll" was upheld.

Government's Cases Weakened by Powell's Advocacy

Due to Powell's *first defense* – delay – he won. The DOJ determined that it would be difficult to successfully prevail at trial given the *decade* that had passed since starting the litigation. They agreed on a settlement basis:

> Land would be restored to full bloods; the cases involving mixed bloods who were competent to sell would be dismissed; and others who were defrauded, such as

minors, would receive the difference between their original payments and the fair value of the property at time of sale, plus six percent interest to the time of settlement [not their land]. Significantly, no remedy was established for mixed bloods who had been defrauded.[28]

Powell ensured that most of his clients' purchases were protected for a comparatively small cost. Nichols-Chisholm paid only $48,497 and its sister firm, Park Rapids Lumber, only $23,015.

Indian Nations – Be Aware of Delay Tactic and When It Will and Will Not Be to Your Benefit

More than 2,000 suits had been filed by the federal government involving over 2,500 allotments and 142,000 acres of land, asserting that White Earth allotments had been wrongfully obtained from both full-bloods and minors. Powell's timber company clients continued logging while the cases were being pursued. As a law clerk in my first semester of law school, the first rule I learned was that if it would benefit my client, delay, delay, delay.

CASE STUDY No. 9: GET MONEY UP FRONT

Given the Pyramid Lake Paiutes' and Walker River Indian Reservations valuable fisheries, it is not surprising that encroachments would be made by white settlers. The non-Indian railroad depot town of Wadsworth had even been established and settled by squatters within the Pyramid Lake Paiutes' Reservation.

In 1891, Com'r T.J. Morgan reported that under Congress' 1892 Indian appropriation act, he was authorized to appoint a commission to negotiate with the Northern Paiutes for a cession of seven miles of the southern end of the Pyramid Lake Reservation, including the town of Wadsworth. However, once a reduction plan is initiated, other players introduce their desires. Suddenly added were (1) cutting-off not only the southern end of the Reservation, but the northern end as well; (2) closing the Walker River Reservation; and (3) concentrating all of the Northern Paiutes on the Pyramid Lake Reservation. The Paiutes were totally opposed to the legislation introduced to accomplish these objectives. Fearing the worst, after seven years, the Pyramid Lake Paiutes agreed to cede the southern end of their Reservation. Congress approved the cession in 1898 (30 Stats., 594). Payment would be provided by white squatters buying the ceded land.

So as not to have to pay, the squatters simply refused to take any legal action to secure title. In the meantime, the town of Wadsworth died as the new owner of the rail line, Southern Pacific, bypassed it for the nearby town of Sparks. Southern Pacific offered the white squatters clear deed to a 50' x 140' lot for the grand sum of $1 in the new town. "To make the deal more enticing, it offered to pick up and move—free of charge—every house in Wadsworth and reassemble it in this new town."[29]

The treasure trove for the Paiutes seven-mile reduction from sales to the citizens of Wadsworth was pirated away.

Indian Nations – Get Money Up Front

In the case of water settlement agreements, payment for needed infrastructure was not worked out in advance but agreements were signed any way, water rights forfeited in some cases and Indians left high and dry. As said by a prominent Indian leader about its water for which there is no delivery system: "It's like a pitcher on a high shelf we can't reach."

CASE STUDY NO. 10: CONDEMNED BACON

General John Pope's admission of the starvation of reservation Indians severely impacted Montana Indians.[30] The Blackfeet Indians endured starvation in the Winters of 1881-1882 and 1883-1884. Men, women and children died.[31] A Special Agent reported the extensive numbers in need of food: Last week 3,200 persons presented themselves as actually in need of subsistence.[32]

Again, as to the Blackfeet:

> *Their supplies had been limited and many of them were gradually dying of starvation.* I visited a large number of their tents and cabins. All bore marks of suffering from lack of food, but *the little children seemed to have suffered most; they were so emaciated that it did not seem possible for them to live long, and many of them have since passed away.* To feed these Indians, I was reduced to such a strait that *I was compelled to issue over 2,000 pounds of bacon which had been condemned.* Indians stripped the bark from saplings to eat. The buffalo, on which these people formerly subsisted, is now extinct. (Emphasis added).[33]

Comment: It is important to remember the courageous Indians who endured the policies of extermination, starvation, exposure, disease, the eradication of everything Indian and the wholesale annihilation of Indian Nations.

Case Study No. 11: Utes Thrown Out of Colorado Due to Meeker and Major Thornburgh

Nathan C. Meeker, White River Ute Reservation Indian Agent, had no experience working with Indians and the White River Utes resented his paternalistic attitudes. He expressed his unfavorable opinions about the Utes in the press and to Nevada's popular Senator Teller: In an article in the Greeley Tribune on Jan. 29, 1879, Meeker wrote: "[They] will not work, neither attach any value to learning ... find occupation and happiness in gambling and horseracing, and the women in both are of no account." In another article he wrote: "They are savages, having no written language, no traditional history, no poetry, no literature ... a race without ambition, and also a race deficient in the inherent elements of progress. *Vermin abound on their persons...*" He reported to CO's influential Senator Teller, "*I propose to cut every Indian down to the bare starvation point* if he will not work." (Emphasis added).

On Sep. 10, 1879, Meeker sent a telegram to Com'r Hayt requesting troops to repress a 'threatened' uprising by the White River Utes after a tribal member shoved him in an argument. Gen. Sherman approved the request and Major Thornburgh was despatched with a force of 153 soldiers and 25 civilians. He was ordered to seek instructions from Agent Meeker.

On Sep. 27, 1879, Meeker sent a letter to Major Thornburgh "to inform you that the Indians are greatly excited, and wish you to *stop at some convenient camping place, and then that you and five soldiers of your command come into the Agency, when a talk and a better understanding can be had. ... The Indians seem to consider the advance of the troops as a declaration of real war. ... The first object is to allay apprehension."* (Emphasis added).[34]

Major Thornburgh *unilaterally* decided that instead of sending a small group to meet with Meeker and the Indians at the Agency, he would enter the Ute Reservation with all of his soldiers.[35] When his forces entered the Ute Reservation, the Utes attacked. For seven days, the soldiers were besieged by the Utes. Thornburgh and thirteen of his men were killed. Other Utes attacked the Indian Agency, killing Agent Meeker, his 10 male employees and taking five women and children captive.

Colorado's Governor Pitkin denounced the attacks in no uncertain terms, and *incidentally* pointed out that 12,000,000 acres could be opened with the removal of the Utes. His War Order No. 1 was to "bring in, dead or alive, all hostile Indians found off the reservation ..."[36]

In order to punish the Utes, they were ordered to appear in Washington, DC. Legislation was forced on them under which their reservations were stripped from them and they were to be removed. The White River Utes were forcibly removed to the Uintah Reservation in Utah. The Uncompahgre Utes were supposed to be removed to lands on the Grand River, in Colorado. Instead, they, too, were forcibly removed to the Uintah Reservation in Utah. The Southern Utes were removed to lands on the La Plata River in Colorado. The military had to use force to keep the whites off the forfeited Uncompahgre Reservation until the Indians were gone.[37] The State of Colorado sought the removal of the Southern Utes to Utah, as well, continuing its efforts through the mid-1890s. They failed and Colorado was left with the Southern Utes remaining on two small reservations in the far southwest corner of the state.

Indian Nations Well Aware of Being Blamed and Punished for Something Not of Their Doing

The government will use any tactic they think will succeed, including blaming the innocent and punishing them, accordingly.

Case Study No. 12: "If You're Not at the Table, You're on the Menu"

On Nov. 3, 1875, a mysterious meeting was convened at the White House with President Grant, Secretary of War Belknap and Generals Sheridan and Crook. Secretary of the Interior Chandler and General Cowen were sent for and the result was that President Grant ordered the military to not oppose miners invading the Black Hills promised to the Lakota in the Treaty of 1868.[38] Grant, the Indian Peace Policy President, would breach the Treaty and instigate war.

They came up with a three-phase plan. First, the DOI would concoct a report with complaints about the Lakotas justifying military action. A report was prepared and leaked to the press within 6 days of the secret meeting. Second, the Lakotas would be ordered to return to their reservation or be attacked by Jan. 31, 1876, a deadline they couldn't meet. The order didn't reach the Standing Rock Agency until December 22, 1875. Agent Burke at Standing Rock requested that the Indians be given an extension of time because of weather conditions but his request was denied. Third, a winter U.S. military campaign would be promptly launched after the expiration of the deadline.[39]

Comment: Keep a prominent Indian leader's advise in mind: "If you're not at the table, you're on the menu."

CASE STUDY NO. 13: LOW BALL

Gold was discovered near the boundary line of the Shoshone Reservation. According to the DOI, "The best gold mines in the district had been found to be located within the reservation." Felix R. Brunot was appointed as a commissioner to negotiate with the Shoshone Indians for the cession of the part of the reservation located in the gold-mining district.

The DOI subsequently reported on the negotiations:

> As a result, **Brunot obtained an agreement from the Shoshones ceding 700,642 acres of the reservation for a total consideration of $27,500 [25 cents/acre]. At that time the Indians had no conception of the value of money or the value of the property they were surrendering to the Government and they accepted, without question, Brunot's first offer of the amount stated**. "Acting upon my experience of the general habit of Indians, the Shoshones were offered a sum as the basis of further negotiation, and which **I supposed would have to be increased to meet the demand of the Indians. When the terms first offered were promptly accepted, I did not feel at liberty to make an addition.**" (Emphasis added).[40]

Indian Nations – Don't Accept the First Offer

Many of us have learned this the hard way. Com'r Leupp had no problem in leaving Indians to the sharp business practices of whites. He stated:

> "[A]s soon as an Indian of either mixed or full blood

becomes capable of taking care of himself, we should set him upon his feet and sever the ties which bind him either to his tribe, in the communal sense, or to the Government. This principle is imperative as to both land and money. ... *[A]fter we have taken our hands off he may fall a victim to sharp practices; but the man never lived-red, white, or any other color-who did not learn a more valuable lesson from one hard blow than from twenty warnings."* (Emphasis added).[41]

The problem is one hard blow could wipe out a whole Indian family's future economic well-being for generations to come.

Case Study No. 14: Polishing a Diamond

The primary duty for the Army of the West was the pacification or defeat of the Indians that fought or resisted westward expansion. In his 1872-1873 Apache Campaign, Gen. Crook used Pima and Maricopa Indian scouts against the Apaches, describing the idea of using Indians against Indians by saying "to polish a diamond there is nothing like its own dust." In recruiting Indian scouts and spies, he declared:

> Nothing breaks them up like turning their own people against them. They don't fear the white soldiers, whom they easily surpass in the peculiar style of warfare which they force upon us, but put upon their trail an enemy of their own blood, an enemy as tireless, as foxy, and as stealthy and familiar with the country as they themselves, and it breaks them all up. It is not merely a question of catching them with Indians, but of a broader and more enduring aim—their disintegration.[42]

The DOI provided intelligence about the Indians to the Army.

Comment: Be wary of any such recruitment among tribal members, which is primary in warfare, commercial or otherwise.

Case Study No. 15: Throwaway Treaty

The Fort Laramie Treaty of 1868 created the Great Sioux Reservation after Red Cloud's victory. Red Cloud demanded the abandonment of Forts Kearney, C.F. Smith and Reno. The U.S. knew the railroad would eliminate the need for the Forts, so it wasn't giving anything up by closing the Forts. General Grant told General Sherman to *abandon the posts and make all the capital with the Indians that can be made out of the change.* By 1868, the railroad terminal at Cheyenne provided direct northward routes to Montana. (Emphasis added). *In brief, the wagon road and the forts through the western hunting grounds of the Teton Sioux were not worth a fight.*[43]

Indian Nations Know that All that Glitters Is Not Gold

The government or corporations are more than willing to give away what they don't want and make Indians think they are getting something, when in reality it is a sham.

CASE STUDY NO. 16: LAND SHARKS

Americans declared that it was their manifest destiny to settle and cultivate America's land from the Atlantic to the Pacific, without regard to Indian rights. Land speculators bought large tracts of land with the expectation that it would quickly increase in value as more people settled in the west and demand increased. It was even better if you could get Indian land cheap and re-sell it for a profit.

Land Speculation and Atchison, Topeka and Santa Fe Railway

Cyrus Holliday secured a charter from the Kansas legislature in 1859 to build the Atchison, Topeka & Santa Fe Railway, but it needed land close to Topeka. Led by Senator Pomeroy, the Railway Company entered into negotiations with the Potawatomi resulting in an 1868 Treaty (15 Stat. 531), approved by Congress, whereby it purchased 338,766 unallotted acres from the Potawatomi at $1 an acre, with easy six-year, 6 percent terms. The Railway Company turned around and put this land on the market to settlers for 20 percent down and the balance in five equal installments. Some tracts were sold for as much as $16 per acre, but others went to insiders like Pomeroy and his brother-in-law at only $1 per acre.[44]

Indian Nations – Beware of Land Sharks

As stated by Commissioner Ezra Hayt:

> "Experience has shown that even the most advanced and civilized of our Indians are not capable of defending their lands when title in fee is once vested in them. The

reservations in such cases are at once infested by a class of land-sharks who do not hesitate to resort to any measure, however iniquitous, to defraud the Indians of their lands."[45]

This could be cited as the "Hayt Rule."

CASE STUDY NO.17: MAYHEM

On Nov. 29, 1864, from in the field at the South Bend of the Big Sandy, John M. Chivington, First Colorado Cavalry, reported as follows:

> In the last ten days my command has marched 300 miles, 100 of which the snow was two feet deep. After a march of forty miles last night *I, at daylight this morning, attacked Cheyenne village of 130 lodges, from 900 to 1,000 warriors strong; killed Chiefs Black Kettle, White Antelope, Knock Knee, and Little Robe [Little Raven], and between 400 and 500 other Indians,* and captured as many ponies and mules. Our loss, 9 killed, 38 wounded. All died nobly. Think I will catch some more of them eighty miles, on Smoky Hill. Found white man's scalp, not more than three days' old, in one of lodges. (Emphasis added).[46]

Yet repeatedly the number of Indians killed has been lowered to 150, even though Col. Chivington reported twice in official recorded War Department messages that he killed 400-500 of them.

In Congressional testimony the mayhem at Sand Creek is vividly described:

> In going over the battle-ground next day I did not see a body of man, woman, or child but was scalped, and in many instances their bodies were mutilated in the most horrible manner—*men, women, and children's privates*

cut out, &c. I heard one man say that he had cut a woman's private parts out, and had them for exhibition on a stick. I heard another man say that he had cut the fingers off of an Indian to get the rings on the hand. According to the best of my knowledge and belief, these atrocities that were committed were with the knowledge of J. M. Chivington, and I do not know of him taking any measures to prevent them. I heard of one instance of a child a few months' old being thrown in the feed-box of a wagon, and after being carried some distance left on the ground to perish. I also heard of numberless instances in which **men had cut out the private parts of females and stretched them over the saddle bows, and wore them over their hats while riding in the ranks**. (Emphasis added).[47]

The volunteer goons fighting against the Walla-Walla Indians in Oregon engaged in the following atrocity:

> **Chief Pu-pu-mux-mux met them under a flag of truce, and declared "He was for peace … He, however, was taken prisoner, and afterwards barbarously murdered, scalped, his ears and hands cut off, and these preserved and sent to the friends of the volunteers in Oregon, all which was reported by volunteers."** (Emphasis added).[48]

Comment: Given names, pursue NAGPRA claims.

CASE STUDY NO. 18: BEWARE THE COMMISSIONER: CHEYENNE AND ARAPAHO THROWN OUT OF COLORADO

A commission was sent to negotiate a treaty with the surviving Arapaho and Cheyenne after the Sand Creek Massacre. Their instructions were as follows: "Agreements to pay money will not be approved. If a treaty is made, it will be one of occupancy only - no title to lands will be acknowledged in the Indians of the country they abandon, nor will any be conferred upon them in the country they are to inhabit..."

On Oct. 13, 1865, the surviving Arapaho and Cheyenne chiefs met with the U.S. treaty commissioners. The Arapaho didn't want to agree on land at the time - few were present, the rest were up north. They were still reeling from the Sand Creek Massacre:

> **Little Raven stated:**
>
> *There is something very strong for us-that fool band of soldiers that cleared out our lodges, and killed our women and children. This is strong (hard) on us. There, at Sand creek, is one chief, Left Hand; White Antelope and many other chiefs lie there; our women and children lie there. Our lodges were destroyed there, and our horses were taken from us there, and I do not feel disposed to go right off in a new country and leave them.* (Emphasis added).[49]

Nonetheless, the Commissioners pressed the Arapaho and Cheyenne to relinquish their Colorado home:

We all fully realize that it is hard for any people to leave their homes and graves of their ancestors; but, **unfortunately for you, gold has been discovered in your country**, and a crowd of white people have gone there to live, and a great many of these people are the worst enemies of the Indians - men who do not care for their interests, and who would not stop at any crime to enrich themselves. These men are now in your country - in all parts of it - and there is no portion where you can live and maintain yourselves but what you will come in contact with them. The consequences of this state of things are that you are in constant danger of being imposed upon, and you have to resort to arms in self defence. ... *We want to give you a country that is full of game and good for agricultural purposes, and where the hills and mountains are not full of gold and silver*. In such a country as this the government can fully provide for your wants ... We are sorry that we have bad people among us, as you are sorry that you have bad people among you; but this is *unfortunately* the case with all people, and however severe we make laws *it is impossible to prevent crime*. You may accede to our wishes, and be happy and prosperous, or you may refuse to make a treaty, and be ruined in health and happiness. (Emphasis added).[50]

Indian Nations: Beware the Commissioner

In a letter from General Crook to Mr. Tibbles, journalist, Indians' rights activist, and politician, Crook stated emphatically that Indians regarded commissioners with something akin to disgust:

> But I am very sorry to say they have, to a very great degree, lost confidence in our people and their promises. Indians are very much like white men in being unable to live upon air. ... *We send them too many commissioners; there is no class of men for whom the Indian has less respect.* (Emphasis added).[51]

Case Study No. 19: "The Lobo"

In January 1859, the New York Times reported on the incendiary convergence of popular opinions, mining schemes, and government policies:

> The Apache is as near the lobo, or wolf of the country, as any human being can be to a beast. ... They neither cultivate nor hunt to any extent, but exist mainly ... by plunder. ... This is the greatest obstacle to the operations of the mining companies. ... [W]hipping these wild tribes ... into submission, and driving them into reservations ... with the penalty of death sternly enforced if they pass their limits, is the only prompt, economical, and humane process. ... My greatest hopes for Arizona, however, rest on the army. ... Officers of various grades are becoming interested in mines throughout that region. They ... have connections of influence and capital.[52]

This type of inflammatory rhetoric ignited vigilante and military campaigns between 1859 and 1874 that killed over 380 Pinal Apaches—including many women and children. Mining across Pinal Apache land followed promptly.[53]

Comment: Ignore these idiots.

CASE STUDY NO. 20: FAKE FRIENDS

When President Lincoln invited Cheyenne and Kiowa leaders to the White House in April 1863, he was seeking to secure peaceful relations with the Indians and to dissuade them from joining forces with the Confederacy.[54] In Colorado, the DOI said it was important to maintain friendly relations with the Utes, for they had the power to stop the development of the great San Juan silver mining district, on and bordering their reservation.[55]

Comment: Keep in mind why an invitation is being extended, instead of being proud.

CASE STUDY NO. 21: KNIGHTS OF THE FOREST

The members of the secret Knights of the Forest took a solemn oath to do everything in their power to remove "all tribes of Indians from the State of Minnesota." A group of them would lie in ambush on the outskirts of the Winnebago Reservation, and shoot any Indian who might be observed outside the lines.[56] The state of terror imposed on Winnebagoes to relinquish their lands is confirmed by the DOI: "The hostile feelings of the white people are so intense that I am necessitated to use extra efforts to keep the Indians upon their own lands, for the reason that *I have been notified by the whites that the Indians will be massacred if they go out of their own country;* and it is but a few days since *a Winnebago was killed* while crossing the Mississippi river for no other reason than that he was an Indian, and such is the state of public opinion that the murderer goes unpunished." (Emphasis added).[57]

Comment: Be alert. These types of groups still exist.

CASE STUDY NO. 22: ONE TREATY PROVISION PERMITTED TRANSCONTINENTAL RAILROAD

Up to 1853 there had been no treaties made with the tribes of the southwest, but in that year Thomas Fitzpatrick, DOI Indian Agent, was **sent as the sole commissioner to make a treaty** of friendship with the Comanche, Kiowa and Apache. A treaty was concluded with them at Fort Atkinson. His interpretation of Article 3 of the Treaty is a clear example of what Peter d'Errico denominates as a **"semantic world created by one group to rule another."**

For the "enterprising" white race, he secured for railroads *"all the concession necessary for locations, pre-emptions, reservations, and settlements, and avoid, besides, the enhanced costs of secondary treaties with those tribes, including, obligating the tribes to enforce rules and regulations prescribed by the federal government."* (Emphasis added).[58]

In 1867, Gen. Sherman wrote to Gen. Ulysses S. Grant, "we are not going to let thieving, ragged Indians check and stop the progress of the railroads." (Emphasis added).[59] Grenville Dodge, Chief Engineer for the Union Pacific Railroad, wrote about the transcontinental railroad: It settles the Indian question, as along its line is the only territory infested by hostile bands of Indians ... as *experience has proved that a railway line through Indian Territory is a fortress as well as a highway.* (Emphasis added).[60]

As the railways expanded, they allowed the rapid transport of troops and supplies to areas where battles were being waged. The DOI wrote:

Indeed, the progress of two years more, if not of another summer, on the Northern Pacific Railroad will of itself completely solve the great Sioux problem, and leave the ninety thousand Indians ranging between the two transcontinental lines as incapable of resisting the Government as are the Indians of New York or Massachusetts. *Columns moving north from the Union Pacific, and south from the Northern Pacific, would crush the Sioux ...* (Emphasis added).[61]

Railroads Spur Western Settlement with Pioneer Vigilantes

In his 1871 Report to the Secretary of the Treasury, the U.S. Commissioner of Mining Statistics, captured the *carte blanche approval for settlers* to deal with the Indians "*in their own way.*"

But what the Government has not been able to do in the past the South Pacific or Texas Pacific Railroad will certainly do. As in the case of the Union and Central Pacific roads, it will attract population, and *the citizens, less hampered in regard to Indians than the military powers, will soon dispose of the question in their own way.* (Emphasis added). ... *Emigration pouring in would soon solve the Indian problem by the extermination or complete subjugation of the hostile tribes.* (Emphasis added).[62]

Professional Hunters Riding Trains Decimate Buffalo, Commissary of Indians

Massive buffalo hunting parties began to arrive in the West by train on excursions for "hunting by rail." By the 1880s, over 5,000 hunters and skinners were involved in the trade.[63]

Frank Hall in his 1895 History of Colorado details this slaughter:

Herds of buffaloes were seen on the eastern plains of Colorado up to 1871, but all have since disappeared, as the commercial spoil of huntsmen and hide gatherers.

The wholesale decimation began in great force and for a distinct purpose—that of collecting hides—in 1869-70. The railways afforded transportation for the hides ($1-2 apiece), heads, and the edible parts of the carcasses. Then came a cloud of bone gatherers, who collected the whitened remnants of skeletons and sold them at five dollars a ton, to be converted into buttons, knife handles, combs and fertilizers. At nearly all the railway stations vast heaps of these bones were stacked up, awaiting shipment to markets east of the Missouri. The Kansas Pacific and Atchison, Topeka & Santa Fe took away hundreds of carloads. "In a little more than three months," says one writer, "in the fall of 1874, over 50,000 hides were shipped from the stations on the Santa Fe road, and it was estimated that the shipments for the year over that and the Kansas Pacific aggregated 125,000. During the winter season of five months about 2,000,000 pounds of buffalo meat were shipped to all parts of the country. At Kansas City large quantities were cured and packed for eastern consumption."[64]

General Sheridan supported it, stating:

"These men have done more in the last two years, and will do more in the next year, to settle the vexed Indian question, than the entire regular army has done in the last forty years. They are destroying the Indians' commissary. And it is a well known fact that an army losing its base of supplies is placed at a great disadvantage. Send them powder and lead, if you will; but for a lasting peace, let them kill, skin and sell until the buffaloes are exterminated. Then your prairies can be covered with speckled cattle." (Emphasis added).[65]

Importance of Legal Counsel

Again, one provision in a Treaty gave the U.S. what it needed, a fortress to fight against the Indians across the U.S. – the Transcontinental Railroad.

As leaders, the ***broad reading*** the government or a corporation may give a provision must be considered in all documents.

Case Study No. 23: Up Against the Wall

Non-Verbal Communication

Every communicative act carries with it nonverbal components. Body actions such as gestures, facial expressions, posture, and eye contact; vocal behaviors such as pitch, loudness, and tempo of the voice; proximity and potential for touch; physical appearance cues such as attractiveness, dress, and grooming; time messages such as pacing and giving undivided attention; and surrounding furnishings and objects all play a part in creating the total communication. Understand that at least someone will always be watching you. The business and law arenas understand the importance of appearance and nonverbal communication. *For example, in their final instructions to a jury, prior to their deliberations, judges tell jurors that they are permitted to use a person's nonverbal responses and cues to determine credibility.*

Appearance Is Key

You will be assessed on appearance, your vehicle, and time of arrival. The way you greet the receptionist, the way you sit in the lobby, and the way you wait, will all have an impact. Be friendly and pleasant. If you need to wait, sit quietly (no phone calls, no cells) and patiently. You must practice just sitting calmly. No outbursts, eye rolling, smirking, snickering or checking your phone or watch. Observers can distinguish movements as short as 1/50 of a second.

Territory

Territory is a key resource: people display status, dominance, and power by owning, controlling, and accessing more, and qualitatively better, territory. This "territory" also includes personal space. Consider where a meeting should be held. Your placement at the meeting table may be such that you are not near an opening, and from their point of view preferably against a wall, or with sunlight obscuring your vision. Literally, you are "up against the wall," trapped or blinded. Soft chairs, soft lighting, room temperature, music and food are to distract you from the business and legal matter at hand. Do not get comfortable. Do not engage in unnecessary conversation. Do not give information away. You are not there to keep the conversation going, to fill any silences in conversation, or to be approved of. Do not interrupt a speaker. Do not exceed the time allowed for speaking or for continuing the meeting beyond the time allocated. Keep your gestures restrained. Powerless speech is defined as including a high frequency of hedges (e.g., "kind of", "like"), hesitations (e.g., "um"), and intensifiers (e.g., "clearly").

Computer

Know how to use any software you will be using ahead of time. Many times, a person will not have checked his equipment ahead of time and there will be a problem. Others will excuse their inability based on age, etc.

If the meeting will be televised, *it is critical to know when the media will start and when the microphone is on*. In a video on the recent case, *Castro-Huerta v. Oklahoma*, the moderator is unaware that the media has started, and she is shown licking her lips, fixing her hair, wiping her nose, fixing her eyeglasses, drinking from a cup, looking around nervously and appearing socially anxious.

Types of Conflicts

Factual: Easy to resolve. Who won the Super Bowl?

Misunderstanding: Person organizing desk, other worker thinks she is leaving and not staying late to help. Resolved when action is understood. Person is not leaving, just getting ready for continuing their work.

Personality: To be avoided. Can't win.

Value Conflict: To be avoided. Political issues, etc.

CASE STUDY NO. 24: INDOCTRINATION

As I studied Indian history, I learned and wrote about the loss of Indian lives, land and resources. It reversed the effects of my indoctrination in our educational system that was deliberately planned and executed to ensure assimilation. It is difficult to accept that the government you have been taught to trust, that is supposed to support and protect you has in fact betrayed you through centuries of abuse. The image of the U.S. that I was taught was an illusion.

Inculcation of Patriotism

Congress passed legislation in 1889 which allowed the Commissioner of Indian Affairs to enforce the school attendance of Indian children by withholding rations and annuities from Indian families whose children were not attending school.[66]

Com'r Morgan published a detailed set of rules for Indian schools which stipulated a uniform course of study and the textbooks which were to be used in the schools. Instruction was to include "love of country, obedience to law, respect for civil rulers, fidelity to official trust, obligations of oaths, the ballot, and other duties involved in good citizenship."[67]

> On the campus of all the more important schools there should be erected a flagstaff, from which should float constantly, in suitable weather, the American flag. In all schools of whatever size and character, supported wholly or in part by the Government, the "Stars and Stripes" should be a familiar object, and students should be taught

to reverence the flag as a symbol of their nation's power and protection.

Patriotic songs should be taught to the pupils, and they should sing them frequently until they acquire complete familiarity with them. Patriotic selections should be committed and recited publicly, and should constitute a portion of the reading exercises.

National holidays: Washington's birthday, Decoration Day, Fourth of July, Thanksgiving, and Christmas-should be observed with appropriate exercises in all Indian schools.[68]

The 8th of February was to be celebrated as Franchise Day. It was on this day that the Dawes Act was signed into law, and the Commissioner felt that this "is worthy of being observed in all Indian schools as the possible turning point in Indian history, the point at which the Indians may strike out from tribal and reservation life and enter American citizenship and nationality."[69]

CASE STUDY NO. 25: THE IRON TRIANGLE

I wrote the following books as I made this historic journey.

The Earth Is Red, The Imperialism of the Doctrine of Discovery (Publisher, Sunstone Press)

In 1823, United States Supreme Court Chief Justice John Marshall, based on his analysis of custom, not precedential law, proclaimed the "Doctrine of Discovery" as the supreme law of the land in the case, *Johnson v. M'Intosh*. This "doctrine" held that whichever European nation first "discovered" land, then not ruled by a Christian prince or people, could claim ownership. From President Washington on it was a foregone conclusion that America's legacy was a continental empire. Indigenous people in this New World, as it was called, were a mere obstacle to be eliminated or moved out of the way of colonial settlers in their westward expansion. The *Johnson* case followed Chief Justice Marshall's earlier opinion in 1810 that states owned all of the land within their boundaries, regardless of whether it was inhabited by indigenous peoples. It led the southern states to sell indigenous land, pass legislation incorporating it into their counties and abrogate indigenous national sovereignty. The federal government faced the real threat of these southern states seceding from the union if their land-grabbing was thwarted. Transforming indigenous peoples to tenants on their land made it easier to breach solemn treaties the government had entered into with sovereign polities. It made it possible to acquire millions and millions of acres of land. What followed was the loss of indigenous lives, land, game and valuable natural resources, along with the federal government imposing brutal economic sanctions and destructive assimilation policies. Thus, the

United States acquired an empire at fire sale, rock-bottom prices, or without compensation at all, facilitated by Chief Justice Marshall's decisions in two heinous, feigned cases.

The Eclipse of the Sun: Lack of American Indian Curriculum in Certain Colorado High Schools (Publisher, Sunstone Press)

The Eclipse of the Sun details the decades-long failure of Colorado public schools to put into practice a Colorado law mandating the inclusion of minority history and contributions, particularly as it affects American Indian children. In 1998, Colorado state lawmakers mandated that American Indian history and culture be included in the curriculum of high schools in Colorado, based on the persistent efforts of Comanche State Senator Suzanne Williams. In 2003, they broadened the law mandating that in order to graduate students must satisfactorily complete a civil government course which includes the history, culture and social contributions of Indians and other groups. Yet tens of thousands of students graduate each year in the state without learning any of the information that is mandated in that single state graduation requirement. The U.S. Civil Rights Commission noted in 2018 that the "lack of appropriate cultural awareness in school curriculum focusing on Native American history or culture" can (1) be harmful to American Indian students; (2) contribute to a negative learning environment; (3) be isolating and limiting; (4) trigger bullying; and (5) result in negative stereotypes across the board. In Colorado, 81% of American Indian students don't meet state math benchmarks, 85% don't meet state science benchmarks, and 70% don't meet state English language benchmarks. Colorado's continuing neglect of Indian students by excluding anything Indian from their education is harmful. The state is denying the rights of Indian students to see themselves in their education, which is necessary to ensure their academic success.

The Iron Triangle: Business, Government, and Colonial Settlers' Dispossession of Indian Timberlands and Timber (Publisher, Sunstone Press)

Congress acknowledged that from "...the beginning, Federal policy toward the Indian was based on the desire to dispossess him of his land." Under the United States' dictatorial "doctrine of discovery," Indians were mere tenants on their land, with no right to the natural resources. The trajectory was clear: removal, cession of millions of acres of land, interment on reservations, allotment of tribal land to individuals to break up tribes, and the sale of those allotments. Disease, starvation, extermination, massacres, private wars and war crimes ensued. *This opened the "inexhaustible mineral, agricultural and natural resources within their dominion" for white exploitation.* Congressional legislation opened the land of the west for $1.25 per acre or at times for free, without buying Indian land, just to get settlers' boots-on-the-ground. Land sharks, in collusion with federal agents, cheated Indians out of their land and timber. Big business used its political and economic clout to assure its control of the country's natural wealth. Lumber barons monopolized the timber industry and set prices. By 1920, three-fifths of the United States' original timber was gone. Indians served as menial laborers for logging companies, cutting timber and peeling bark. "Scalped" of the wealth inherent in their natural resources, they were left destitute.

All That Glitters Is Ours: The Theft of Indian Mineral Resources (Publisher, Sunstone Press)

The Indians possessed an abundant natural resource environment which included (1) renewable natural resources such as timber, water and arable land, along with wildlife resources such as fish and game; and (2) non-renewable natural resources, such as gold, silver, copper, iron ore, coal and oil. The deliberate policy of the U.S., the Indians' trustee, was to expropriate Indian mineral resources.

The wealth embodied in natural resources was the key component in Indian lands that aggravated the greed of colonial settlers and businesses. The immediacy of revenues that could be derived from natural resources was undeniable. A study by the U.S. Geological Survey in 1923 is very specific as to the value of minerals in Colorado, alone. *The total gross value of Colorado's gold, silver, copper, lead and zinc was calculated to be $1,531,000,000 from 1859-1923*. (Emphasis added).[70]

The U.S., as trustee of Indian lands and resources, faced a huge conflict of interest: revenue was needed to pay off the national debt from the Civil War and to aid in the reconstruction of the south. It was needed to fund the industrial engine that would make the U.S. a dominant world power. Indians were a mere obstacle to subdue through all the brutality imaginable. Combat would be conducted by a technologically superior Army, by vigilante forces armed by the government, by miners and by colonial settlers. Indian country was invaded and Indians incarcerated on reservations.

While Indians were lied to about the value of their lands, mining tycoons became wealthy from producing their minerals. Indians starved to death, froze to death, died from imported diseases and were wantonly exterminated while the Millionaires Club of the Washoe in Nevada was formed by the elite gentlemen of the Comstock in the 1870s, the hey-day of the mining activity, termed the "Silver Seventies."

The U.S. Army used the methods outlined by Prussian General and military theorist Carl von Clausewitz: The *first* of these is invasion, that is the seizure of enemy territory; not with the object of retaining it but in order to exact financial contributions, or even to lay it waste. The immediate object here is neither to conquer the enemy country nor to destroy its army, but simply to cause general damage. The *second* method is to give priority to operations that will increase the enemy's suffering. The *third*, and far the most important method, judging from the frequency of its use, is to wear down the enemy. ... Wearing down the enemy in a conflict means using the duration of the war to bring about a gradual exhaustion of his physical and moral resistance.[71]

Lieutenant General John M. Schofield, commander of the Department of Missouri from 1869 to 1870, stated his career goal as follows: "With my cavalry and combined artillery encamped in front, I wanted no other occupation in life than to ward off the savage and kill off his food until there should no longer be an Indian Frontier in our beautiful country."[72]

Titans of Industry

The titans of industry gathered to wine and dine Prince Henry of Prussia at the Waldorf Astoria in New York City on February 26, 1902. The banquet was attended by more than twelve hundred statesmen, financiers, railroad industry, miners, steel, iron industry, petroleum, timber executives, transportation executives, scientists, inventors, American Society of Mechanical Engineers laureates, telegraphic communications, ship building, tobacco, sugar refining, brewing industry, academics, military officers, and other public men.[73]

Conclusion

I hope this list of historical examples is meaningful today. I had not learned about them until I begin my study of Indian history. The absence of Indian education in our school system is not an accident. It is assimilation at work.

NOTES

Introduction

1. Address by General John Pope before the Social Science Association, at Cincinnati, Ohio, May 24, 1878.

Case Study No. 1: Doctrine of Discovery

2. Letter from Brinton to Ingersoll, 02/26/1822. Illinois Wabash Land Company. https://digital.libraries.ou.edu/IWLC/paper. asp?pID=52&doc_type=Corr (accessed online November 14, 2020).

3. *Johnson v. M'Intosh*, 21 U.S. 543, 574 (1823).

4. "From Thomas Jefferson to William Johnson, 12 June 1823," *Founders Online,* National Archives, https://founders.archives.gov/documents/Jefferson/98-01-02-3562 (accessed online November 12, 2020).

5. Joint Statement of the Dicasteries for Culture and Education and for Promoting Integral Human Development on the "Doctrine of Discovery", 30.03.2023. https://press.vatican.va/content/salastampa/en/bollettino/pubblico/2023/03/30/230330b.html (accessed online April 3, 2023).

6. Canon Law - Precision and Certitude: Laws Governing Laws, September-October 2008, SR. PATRICIA SMITH, OSF, Ph.D., J.C.D. Sr. Smith is assistant professor of pastoral and theological studies, Neumann College, Aston, PA. https://www.chausa.org/publications/health-progress/article/september-october-2008/canon-law—-precision-and-certitude-laws-governing-laws (accessed online April 11, 2023).

7. Chains of Title: how the Vatican shackled post-revolutionary America. David J. MacKinnon and Dr. Sandra J.T.M. Evers.

http://longmarchtorome.com/chains-of-title-how-the-vatican-shackled-post-revolutionary-america/ (accessed online April 11, 2023).

8. https://encyclopediavirginia.org/entries/inter-caetera-by-pope-alexander-vi-may-4-1493/ (accessed online April 11, 2023).

Case Study No. 2: The Starving Rabbit

9. Montana lawmaker wants to revisit idea of reservations. Amy Beth Hanson, January 6, 2023. https://apnews.com/article/politics-new-mexico-state-government-montana-18a03c0ddfd911 64d80d9b67390a8cce (accessed online March 14, 2023).

A JOINT RESOLUTION OF THE SENATE AND THE HOUSE OF REPRESENTATIVES OF THE STATE OF MONTANA URGING CONGRESS TO INVESTIGATE ALTERNATIVES TO THE AMERICAN INDIAN RESERVATION SYSTEM.

WHEREAS, the Indian reservation system was created in a different time and place and under circumstances that no longer exist and is therefore inadequate for the conditions that are present in our state (and nation) in today's world; and

WHEREAS, the Indian reservation system has clearly failed to positively enhance the lives and well-being of most of the Indians or the other citizens of the State of Montana; and

WHEREAS, for most of our Indian citizens, the Indian reservation system has produced the negative effects of drug abuse, alcoholism, domestic violence, welfare dependence, poverty, and substandard educational achievements, resulting in lack of opportunity for their future well-being and happiness; and

WHEREAS, Indian tribes that do not individually own their property have the highest poverty rate of any ethnic group in America; and

WHEREAS, Indian tribes that do not individually own their property have the lowest life expectancy of any ethnic group in America; and

WHEREAS, the Indian reservation system is a policy based entirely on race, which is diametrically opposed to both the United States Constitution and the Constitution of the State of Montana; and

WHEREAS, the Indian reservation system is a policy conferring "sovereign nation" status to individual tribes inside of the borders of the United States, a policy that is, again, diametrically opposed to the Constitution of the United States; and

WHEREAS, previous judicial decisions relative to the reservation system in Montana have produced confusion, acrimony, and animosity among the general population in the past and at present, and will undoubtedly continue to do so in the foreseeable future; and

WHEREAS, the continuation of the reservation system is not in the best interests of either the Indians inside our borders or for our common Montana citizens; and

WHEREAS, we believe the investigation of alternative ways of approaching the reservation system can and will produce a new system that will enhance the lives, the happiness, and the opportunities for our Indian citizens while at the same time promoting peace, harmony, and stability for all.

10. Laws of the Territory of Arizona, Twelfth Legislative Assembly, Also, Memorials and Resolutions, Arizona Miner Steam-Printing Office, 1883, p. 374.

11. Annual Report of the Department of the Interior, Vol. II, Report of the Commissioner of Indian Affairs, Office of Indian Affairs, United States. U.S. Government Printing Office, 1916, p. 58.

Case Study No. 3: The White Shoe Law Firm

12. Paul Weiss Can Bill Oklahoma Up to $1.4 Million in Tribal Case, Kimberly Strawbridge Robinson, May 12, 2022. https://news.bloomberglaw.com/us-law-week/paul-weiss-can-bill-oklahoma-up-to-1-4-million-in-tribal-case (accessed online March 14, 2023).

Case Study No. 4: "Whiskey Is for Drinking, Water Is for Fighting"

13. Report of the Commissioner of Indian Affairs to the Secretary of the Interior, United States. Office of Indian Affairs. U.S. Government Printing Office, 1876, p. 117.

Case Study No. 5: "This Isn't the 15th Century"

14. https://www.chicagotribune.com/news/environment/ct-climate-change-northwest-passage-20170729-story.html (accessed online November 29, 2020).

15. https://globalnews.ca/news/5256532/northwest-passage-canada-us-claim-challenge/ (accessed online November 29, 2020).

16. Doctrine of Discovery, Used for Centuries to Justify Seizure of Indigenous Land, Subjugate Peoples, Must Be Repudiated by United

Nations, Permanent Forum Told, May 8, 2012, United Nations, Economic and Social Council HR/5088, Department of Public Information, News and Media Division, New York, Permanent Forum on Indigenous Issues, Eleventh Session. https://www.un.org/press/en/2012/hr5088.doc.htm (accessed online November 8, 2020).

17. https://uk.reuters.com/article/uk-russia-arctic-canada-idUKN0246498520070802 (accessed online November 8, 2020).

Case Study No. 6: The 'Lost' Shoreline

18. US Congress, Senate, Committee on Interior and Insular Affairs. Providing for the Use of Lands in the Garrison Dam Project by the Three Affiliated Tribes of the Fort Berthold Reservation. 87th Cong., 2d sess., S. Rep. 1723. July 12, 1962.

> 1. Should the grant be in terms of a right or a privilege? We recommend that it be in the terms of a *privilege*. [Language added for this purpose: TAT was *"permitted to graze stock,"* it was given a *"grant of grazing privileges."*] The reason the DOI wanted the grant to be one of privilege and not of a right is as follows: ***Privileges are conditional, subject to change or outright removal by those in authority controlling them.***
>
> 2. Should the grazing privilege be subject to the needs of the flood control project? We believe that it should.
>
> 3. Should the grazing privilege be limited to use by the Indians themselves, or should the Indians be authorized to lease the lands for grazing purposes? We recommend the latter. [Language added for this purpose: leasing to members or nonmembers of the tribes permitted *"on such terms and conditions as the Secretary of the Interior may prescribe"*].
> 4. Should the grazing privilege be limited to a period of 5 years? No.
> 5. Should the grazing privilege be exclusive, or should it be limited to lands that are not devoted to some other beneficial use by the Department of the Army (such as recreation)? [Language added for this purpose: it was limited to former *Indian* land as the *Secretary of the Army determines* is not devoted to other beneficial uses...]
> 6. Should the grazing privilege be limited to lands acquired from the Indians, or should it also apply to project lands within the reservation that were acquired from non-Indians? We recommend the latter. [***THIS WAS NOT INCLUDED*** in the final legislation as it would have applied to non-Indian owned land within the Reservation.]
> 7. The closing sentence was to protect existing grazing leases and permits. It would require "due diligence" —a search for the "existing" grazing leases and permits to determine what was already in force, which did not occur.

19. Berman, Terri. "For the Taking: The Garrison Dam and the Tribal

Taking Area," February 22, 2010. https://www.culturalsurvival.org/
publications/cultural-survival-quarterly/taking-garrison-dam-and-tribal-
taking-area (accessed online March 14, 2023).

Case Study No. 7: Last Arrow

20. https://www.ndstudies.gov/curriculum/high-school/standing-rock-
oyate/documents-standing-rock (accessed online April 9, 2023).

Representative of department speaking:

The President of the United States has sent me to speak a solemn and serious
word to you, a word that means more to some of you than any other that you
have ever heard. He has been told that there are some among you who should
no longer be controlled by the Bureau of Indian Affairs, but should be given
their patents in fee and thus become free American citizens. It is his decision
that this shall be done, and that those so honored by the people of the United
States shall have the meaning of this new and great privilege pointed out by
symbol and by word, so that no man or woman shall not know its meaning.
The President has sent me papers naming those men and women and I shall
call out their names one by one, and they will come before me.

For Men:

(Read Name.)

_____ (white name). What was your Indian name? (Gives
name.)

_____ (Indian name). I hand you a bow and an arrow. Take
this bow and shoot the arrow. (He shoots.)

_____ (Indian name). You have shot your last arrow. That
means that you are no longer to live the life of an Indian. You are from this day
forward to live the life of the white man. But you may keep that arrow, it will
be to you a symbol of your noble race and of the pride you feel that you come
from the first of all Americans.

_____ (white name). Take in your hand this plow. (He takes
the handles of the plow.) This act means that you have chosen to live the life of
the white man—and the white man lives by work. From the earth we all must
get our living and the earth will not yield unless man pours upon it the sweat
of his brow. Only by work do we gain a right to the land or to the enjoyment
of life.

_____ (white name). I give you a purse. This purse will always
say to you that the money you gain from your labor must be wisely kept. The
wise man saves his money so that when the sun does not smile and the grass
does not grow, he will not starve.

I give into your hands the flag of your county. This is the only flag you have
ever had or ever will have. It is the flag of freedom; the flag of free men, the flag
of a hundred million free men and women of whom you are now one. That
flag has a request to make of you, _____ (white name), that

you take it into your hands and repeat these words:

"For as much as the President has said that I am worthy to be a citizen of the United States, I now promise to this flag that I will give my hands, my head, and my heart to the doing of all that will make me a true American citizen." And now beneath this flag I place upon your breast the emblem of your citizenship. Wear this badge of honor always; and may the eagle that is on it never see you do aught of which the flag will not be proud.

(The audience rises and shouts: "_____(white name) is an American citizen.")

For Women:

_____ (white name). Take in your hand this work bag and purse. (She takes the work bag and purse.)

This means that you have chosen the life of the white woman—and the white woman loves her home. The family and the home are the foundation of our civilization. Upon the character and industry of the mother and homemaker largely depends the future of our Nation. The purse will always say to you that the money you gain from your labor must be wisely kept. The wise woman saves her money, so that when the sun does not smile and the grass does not grow, she and her children will not starve.

I give into your hands the flag of your country. This is the only flag you have ever had or ever will have. It is the flag of freedom, the flag of free men, a hundred million free men and women of whom you are now one. That flag has a request to make of you, _____ (white name), that you take it into your hands and repeat these words:

"For as much as the President has said that I am worthy to be a citizen of the United States, I now promise to this flag that I will give my hands, my head, and my heart to the doing of all that will make me a true American citizen." And now beneath this flag I place upon your breast the emblem of your citizenship. Wear this badge of honor always, and may the eagle that is on it never see you do aught of which the flag will not be proud.

(The audience rises and shouts: "_____(white name) is an American citizen.")

21. http://savagesandscoundrels.org/people/savages-scoundrels/chief-old-dog/ (accessed online November 20, 2020).
22. *Ex parte Green*, 123 F.2d 862 (2d Cir. 1941).

Case Study No. 8: Skull Studies

23. Moorehead, Warren King. The American Indian in the United States, Period 1850-1914. Andover MA: Andover Press, 1914, pp. 73, 75.
24. William W. Folwell, History of Minnesota, rev. ed. (St. Paul:

Minnesota Historical Society, 1969), 4: 278-279.

25. Report of the Commissioner of Indian Affairs to the Secretary of the Interior, United States. Office of Indian Affairs, U.S. Government Printing Office, 1911, p. 42.

26. Report of the Commissioner of Indian Affairs to the Secretary of the Interior, United States. Office of Indian Affairs, U.S. Government Printing Office, 1912, p. 43.

27. Peterson, Ken. "Ransom Powell and the Tragedy of White Earth." Minnesota History 63.3 (2012): 96.

28. Id.

Case Study No. 9: Get Money Up Front

29. https://www.up.com/goldenspike/sacramento-promontory.html (accessed online March 16, 2023).

Case Study No. 10: Condemned Bacon

30. Address by General Pope before the Social Science Association, at Cincinnati, Ohio, May 24, 1878. Delivered by Request of the Association (Cincinnati: n.p., 1878).

31. Report of the Commissioner of Indian Affairs to the Secretary of the Interior, United States. Office of Indian Affairs. U.S. Government Printing Office, 1881, p. XV.

32. Report of the Commissioner of Indian Affairs to the Secretary of the Interior, Vol. 2, United States. Office of Indian Affairs. U.S. Government Printing Office, 1884, p. 151.

33. Id.

Case Study No. 11: Utes Thrown Out of Colorado due to Meeker and Major Thornburgh

34. Elmer R. Burkey, "The Thornburgh Battle With the Utes on Milk River," The Colorado Magazine 13 (May 1936): 93.

35. War Department, General of the Army, Annual Report of the Secretary of War (1880).

> Major Thornburgh unilaterally decided that instead of sending a small group to meet with Meeker as Meeker and the Indians personally requested of him, he would enter the Reservation with all of his soldiers, fearing trouble. He sent Agent Meeker the following message:
> *I have, after due deliberation, decided to modify my plans:* ... I shall

move with my entire command to some convenient camp near, and within striking distance of your agency, reaching such point during the 29th. ... *I have carefully considered whether or not it would be advisable to have my command at a point as distant as that desired by the Indians who were in camp last night*, and have reached the conclusion that under my orders, which require me to march this command to the agency, *I am not at liberty to leave it at a point where it would not be available in case of trouble*. (Emphasis added).

36. U.S. Congress, House, Extinguishment of Indian Title, 46th Cong., 1st sess., Congressional Record, vol. 9, pt. l, 21 April 1880, 615.

37. Annual Reports of the Secretary of War, Volume 1, United States. War Department, 1881, p. 116.

Case Study No. 12: "If You're Not at the Table, You're on the Menu"

38. Gray, John Stephens. Centennial Campaign: The Sioux War of 1876, Vol. 8. University of Oklahoma Press, 1988, p. 26.

39. Military expedition against the Sioux Indians, July 18, 1876, H.R. Exec. Doc. No. 184, 44th Cong., 1st Sess. (1876).

Case Study No. 13: Low Ball

40. Report of the Commissioner of Indian Affairs to the Secretary of the Interior, United States. Office of Indian Affairs. U.S. Government Printing Office, 1872, p. 126. H.R. Exec. Doc. No. 1, 42nd Cong., 3rd Sess. (1872).

41. Outlook and Independent, Volume 94, *Library of American civilization,* Outlook Publishing Company, p. 957.

Case Study No. 14: Polishing a Diamond

42. Charles F. Lummis, General Crook and the Apache Wars (Flagstaff, AZ, 1966), p. 17.

Case Study No. 15: Throwaway Treaty

43. Grant to Sherman, March 2, 1868, Letters Sent, Commanding General, NA, RG 108.

Case Study No. 16: Land Sharks

44. Railroads of Kansas. Kathy Alexander, Feb. 2023. https://legendsofkansas.com/kansas-railroads/ (accessed online March 14, 2023).

45. Report of the Commissioner of Indian Affairs to the Secretary of the Interior, United States. Office of Indian Affairs, U.S. Government Printing Office, 1878, pp. VIII-X.

Case Study No. 17: Mayhem
46. The War of the Rebellion: A Compilation of the Official Records of the Union and Confederate Armies, United States War Department, U.S. Government Printing Office, 1891. Series I, Vol. XLI, Part I, LOUISIANA AND THE TRANS-MISSISSIPPI, Chapter LIIIO, p. 948.
47. Condition of the Indian Tribes: Report of the Joint Special Committee, Appointed Under Joint Resolution of March 3, 1865, United States. Congress. Joint Special Committee to Inquire into the Condition of the Indian Tribes, Kraus Reprint Company, 1973, p. 57.
48. Indian hostilities in Oregon and Washington. Message from the President of the United States, communicating information relative to Indian hostilities in the Territories of Oregon and Washington, H.R. Rep. No. 93, 34th Cong., 1st Sess. (1856), p. 33.

Case Study No. 18: Beware the Commissioner: Cheyenne and Arapaho Thrown Out of Colorado
49. Report of the Commissioner of Indian Affairs to the Secretary of the Interior, United States. Office of Indian Affairs. U.S. Government Printing Office, 1865, p. 525.
50. Ibid., p. 523.
51. George Crook, The Council Fire 2, No. 12 (December 1879): 178-79.

Case Study No. 19: "The Lobo"
52. Welch, J. R. (2017). Earth, Wind, and Fire: Pinal Apaches, Miners, and Genocide in Central Arizona, 1859-1874. SAGE Open, 7(4).
53. Annihilationist Government Policy and Miner Bombast Targeting Pinal Apaches
        Welch, J. R. (2017). Earth, Wind, and Fire: Pinal Apaches, Miners, and Genocide in Central Arizona, 1859-1874. SAGE Open, 7(4).

Date and Source	Statement(s) (Emphasis added).
October 26, 1864 ("Apache rangers" 1864, p. 1, col. 2)	"a bill ... adopted by the Legislature, authorizing the raising of not more than six companies of rangers to fight Apaches. ... [I]f we do not conquer the savages they will ... drive us from the country. ... *Extermination is our only hope, and the sooner it is accomplished the better* ... Let the necessary work go on."
October 31,1865 (Farish, 1916, Vol. 4, p. 126)	General John S. Mason, issues General Order No. 11: *"All Apache Indians in this Territory are hostile and all men old enough to bear arms who are encountered will be slain.* ... All rancherias, provisions and whatever of value belonging to the Indians ... will be destroyed."
September 22, 1868 (Major General H. W. Halleck, 1869, p. 49)	"The Apaches ... are the natural and hereditary enemies of the whites. ... They have successfully expelled from that Territory the Aztecs, the Spaniards and the Mexicans; and they will yield to our people only when compelled to do so by the rifle. ... Murder and robbery constitute almost the sole occupation of the Apaches ... plundering and destroying unprotected agricultural and mining settlements. ... They will observe no treaties, agreements, or truces. *With them there is no alternative but active and vigorous war, till they are completely destroyed."*
September 27, 1869 (General Order, 1870, pp. 121-122)	"On taking command of the department I was satisfied that the few settlers and scattered miners of Arizona were the sheep upon which these wolves habitually preyed . ... *I encouraged the troops to capture and root out the Apache by every means, and to hunt them as they would wild animals*. ... over two hundred have been killed, generally by parties who have trailed them for days and weeks ... lying in wait for them by day and following them by night. Many villages have been burned, large quantities of arms and supplies of ammunition, clothing and provisions have been destroyed. ... Some of the bands, having the fear of extermination before them, have sued for peace."
January 23, 1871 ("The Pacific Coast," 1871, p. 1)	*"Governor Safford . . . recommends a war of extermination against Apache Indians, and favors the employment of volunteers composed of settlers ... as more effective and cheaper than regular troops."*
August 26, 1871 ("Indian War in Arizona," 1871, p. 1)	"Crook is bent on exerting the fullest strength of his command to punish hostile Indians. ... The Territory will be scoured as it never has been, and the Apaches warred upon in a manner that will strike them with awe, and we believe produce an early peace."
September 26, 1871 ("The Indians: The Campaign," 1871, p. 1)	"Governor Sofford [sic] and a company of 200 miners and Indian hunters had found rich gold placers in the Pinal country, and were still scouting after gold and Apaches."
March 30, 1872 ("Arizona,"1872, p. 1)	"not only mining, but all classes of industry are seriously hindered by the atrocities of the murderous Apaches. ... Peaceable miners in the pursuit of their vocation are shot down, pick and shovel in hand. ... *The inhabitants saw a glimmer of hope in the arrival of General Crook, whose policy is to exterminate the Indians entirely as the most efficient means of making peace with them."*

Case Study No. 20: Fake Friends
54. Washington National Republican, March 27, 1868.
55. Report of the Commissioner of Indian Affairs, Department of the Interior, United States. Office of Indian Affairs, U.S. Government Printing Office, 1890, p. vi.

Case Study No. 21: Knights of the Forest
56. Mankato Review, April 27, 1886; Mankato Daily Review, April 18, 1916. Coats, Catherine M., "Extermination or Removal: The Knights of the Forest and Ethnic Cleansing in Early Minnesota" (2017). Culminating Projects in History, p. 62. https://repository.stcloudstate.edu/hist_etds/11 (accessed online April 21, 2022).
57. Report of the Commissioner of Indian Affairs to the Secretary of the Interior, United States. Office of Indian Affairs. U.S. Government Printing Office, 1863, p. 92.

Case Study No. 22: One Treaty Provision Permitted Transcontinental Railroad
58. Sen. doc. No. 1. pt. 1. ls. 330. p. 363. Pub. doc. No. 690.
> *[I]n view of the fact that at no distant day the whole country over which those Indians now roam must be peopled by another and more enterprising race...* [and that] a great central route to the Pacific by railway has become deeply impressed upon the public mind; and while many courses are contemplated two of them at least are designed to pass through this section of the country. [T]he acknowledgment contained in [Article 3] may be found of inestimable value. *It will afford all the concession necessary for locations, pre-emptions, reservations, and settlements, and avoid, besides, the enhanced costs of secondary treaties with those tribes.* (Emphasis added).

59. The Papers of Ulysses S. Grant: January 1-September 30, 1867. Volume 17 of Papers of Ulysses S. Grant, Ulysses Simpson Grant, Editor John Y. Simon, SIU Press, 1991, p. 162.
60. Report of Gen. G. M. Dodge, Chief Engineer, 1874, Grenville M. Dodge, 1880, p. 48.
61. Report of the Commissioner of Indian Affairs to the Secretary of the Interior, United States. Office of Indian Affairs. U.S. Government Printing Office, 1872, p. 9.
62. Statistics Of Mines And Mining In The States And Territories West Of The Rocky Mountains: Being The 6th Annual Report Of U.S. Commissioner Of Mining Statistics to Secretary of Treasury,

1871, pp. 278, 280.

63. "Buffalo Hunting: Shooting Buffalo From the Trains of the Kansas Pacific Railroad," Harper's Weekly, December 14, 1867.

Nearly every railroad train which leaves or arrives at Fort Hays on the Kansas Pacific Railroad has its race with these herds of buffalo; and a most interesting and exciting scene is the result. *The train is "slowed" to a rate of speed about equal to that of the herd; the passengers get out fire-arms which are provided for the defense of the train against the Indians, and open from the windows and platforms of the cars a fire that resembles a brisk skirmish.* Frequently a young bull will turn at bay for a moment. His exhibition of courage is generally his death-warrant, for the whole fire of the train is turned upon him, either killing him or some member of the herd in his immediate vicinity. (Emphasis added).

64. Hall, Frank. History of the State of Colorado, Embracing Accounts of the Pre-historic Races and Their Remains: The Earliest Spanish, French and American Explorations... the First American Settlements Founded; the Original Discoveries of Gold in the Rocky Mountains; the Development of Cities and Towns, with the Various Phases of Industrial and Political Transition, from 1858 to 1890... Vol. 4. Blakely Printing Company, 1895, p. 355.

65. Buffalo Hunters. https://www.legendsofamerica.com/we-buffalohunters/ (accessed online February 18, 2023).

Case Study No. 23: Up Against the Wall
None

Case Study No. 24: Indoctrination

66. Report of the Commissioner of Indian Affairs to the Secretary of the Interior, Office of Indian Affairs. U.S. Government Printing Office, 1890, p. viii.

67. Ibid., p. CLIX.

68. Ibid., p. CLXVII.

69. Ibid., p. CLXVIII.

Case Study No. 25: The Iron Triangle

70. MINING IN COLORADO A HISTORY OF DISCOVERY, DEVELOPMENT AND PRODUCTION BY CHARLES W. HENDERSON, DEPARTMENT OF THE INTERIOR, Hubert Work, Secretary, U.S. GEOLOGICAL SURVEY, George Otis Smith, Director, Professional Paper 138, Washington Government Printing Office, 1926, p. 249.

71. Von Clausewitz, Carl. On war. Vol. 1. Jazzybee Verlag, 1950.

72. John M. Schofield, Forty-six years in the Army, 1869, p. 428. https://www.perseus.tufts.edu/hopper/text?doc=Perseus:text:2001.05.0131 (accessed online April 3, 2023).

9 781632 936523